This Book Belongs To:

_____

_____

My First Yoga™
Animal Poses

By Abbie Davies

My First Yoga: Animal Poses
ISBN 978-0-9826559-0-0

In order to ensure a safe, enjoyable experience consult
with a physician before commencing any exercise.

Illustrations by Mark Dormand
Art Direction and Design by Trevor Steinbacher

For information address:
My First Yoga
P.O. Box 400398, Cambridge, MA 02140
www.myfirstyoga.com

First Edition

Introduction

This book uses kid friendly vocabulary and vibrant illustrations to lead readers through a series of easy to follow yoga poses. Learn to become a strong dog, quiet turtle and proud lion— stretching mind and body to improve focus, balance and concentration.

Yoga is a unique type of exercise that helps to prepare our minds and bodies for many of the activities that we do each day. Throughout this book we have singled out one major benefit, along with a few common relatable kid's activities, for each featured yoga pose. It is our hope that the listed benefits and activities help to connect readers to poses.

While this book is designed to engage even the youngest of readers, don't be afraid to join in on the fun!

Begin with a warm-up by sitting on a carpeted floor or mat with plenty of space and away from distractions. Before and after each exercise, relax by taking a few slow, deep breaths through your nose.

Now lets get started...

Monkey

Monkey Pose

Improves Concentration (Student/Musician/Artist)

Sit down on your bottom criss-cross. Sit up tall with your shoulders and bring one hand in front of your belly. Breathe in and stretch one arm up to the sky and with a quick, powerful breath bring your hand back down. HA! Now switch.

Giraffe

Giraffe Pose

Strengthens Legs (Soccer/Skiing/Cycling)

Stand up tall and jump your feet apart. Bend your knees and elbows.
Bring one of your elbows down to your knee and stretch your opposite
arm up to the sky to make your long giraffe neck. This giraffe is hungry,
munch on some leaves high up in the trees. MUNCH! MUNCH! MUNCH!

Flamingo

Flamingo Pose

Improves Balance (Gymnastics/Dancing)

Stand up tall and tuck your hands under your shoulders like wings. Bend one knee and lift it up off of the ground. Try balancing like a flamingo while you count to five. Then switch legs.

Dog

Dog Pose

Strengthens Arms & Legs (Tennis/Football/Running)

Kneel down on your knees. Stretch your paws wide and place them on the ground in front of you. Now look at your toes and lift your tail up to the sky. Wag your dog tail side to side. Take three slow, deep breaths. Can you lift one leg up to the sky? Switch!

Cat

Cat Pose

Stretches Upper Body (Basketball/Golf/Lacrosse)

Place your hands and knees on the ground. Press into your cat paws, gently tuck your chin to your chest and look up toward your belly button as you arch your back. Slowly tilt your tail from side to side as you MEOW like a cat.

Cow

Cow Pose

Stretches Upper Body (Baseball/Rugby/Karate)

Place your hands and knees on the ground. Press into your cow hooves as you drop your belly down toward the ground and lift your head up to the sky. MOO!

Snake

Sssss

Snake Pose

Strengthens Spine (Swimming/Diving)

Lay down on your belly and hide in some tall grass. Put your hands on the ground underneath your shoulders and use your strong arms to lift your head and shoulders up off the ground. Sssssss!

Lion

ROAAR

Lion Pose

Strengthens Face, Mouth & Throat (Singers/Actors)

Kneel down with your toes together and knees apart. Spread your paws wide and glue them to your knees. Puff up your lion chest. Take a big breath in and ROAR!!!

Butterfly

Butterfly Pose

Stretches Hips (Snowboarding/Hockey/Surfing)

Sit down, bend your knees and bring the bottoms of your feet together. Sit up tall with your shoulders and bring your hands to your feet. Breathe in as you flap your wings up and breathe out as you flap your wings down. Can you stretch your nose to your toes?

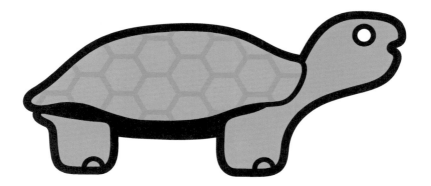

Turtle

Turtle Pose

Relaxes Mind & Body (Everyone)

Sit down, bend your knees and bring the bottoms of your feet together.
Place your hands in-between your knees and stretch your arms underneath
your knees. Bend forward and bring your nose to your toes to hide inside
your turtle shell. Count to three then lift your head up. PEEK-A-BOO!

Namaste

Strengthens Connections (Self/Family/Freinds)

Sit down on your bottom criss-cross. Bring your hands together as you say the word 'Namaste.' Namaste means, 'I am nice to you, and you are nice to me'.

Turtle

Monkey

Giraffe

Butterfly

Animal Poses

Flamingo

Lion

Dog

Snake

Cow

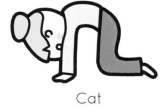

Cat

CPSIA information can be obtained
at www.ICGtesting.com
Printed in the USA
LVIC041307280612

288039LV00003B